THE DOWNWARD SPIRALS

36 Minute Major

BY
JOHN
SIMCOE

THE DOWNWARD SPIRALS
36 Minute MAJOR
(COLLECTION 2)

WWW.DOWNWARDSPIRALS.COM

ISBN-13: 978-0692724569 (Parade of Heroes)

ISBN-10: 0692724567

Previous DOWNWARD SPIRALS Books by JOHN SIMCOE:
- DOWNWARD SPIRALS VOLUME 1: TWISTED TAILS
- DOWNWARD SPIRALS: FREE? WHO ARE THEY KIDDING?

MORE BY JOHN SIMCOE:
- TOMMY ONE and the APOCALYPSE GUN (Pro Se Press)
- LEGENDS OF NEW PULP FICTION (Airship 27)
- G.I. JOE: SCOURGE OF THE AMAZON (Kindle Worlds)
- DUNGEON MAGAZINE Nos. 105, 110, 118 (Paizo Publishing)
- D6 SPACE: ALIENS VOLUME 1 (West End Games)
- FACTION FOLIO 1: THE LABYRINTH (EN Publishing)
- FACTION FOLIO 2: THE BLACKCLOAK WATCH (EN Publishing)
- REDLIGHTER

THE DOWNWARD SPIRALS

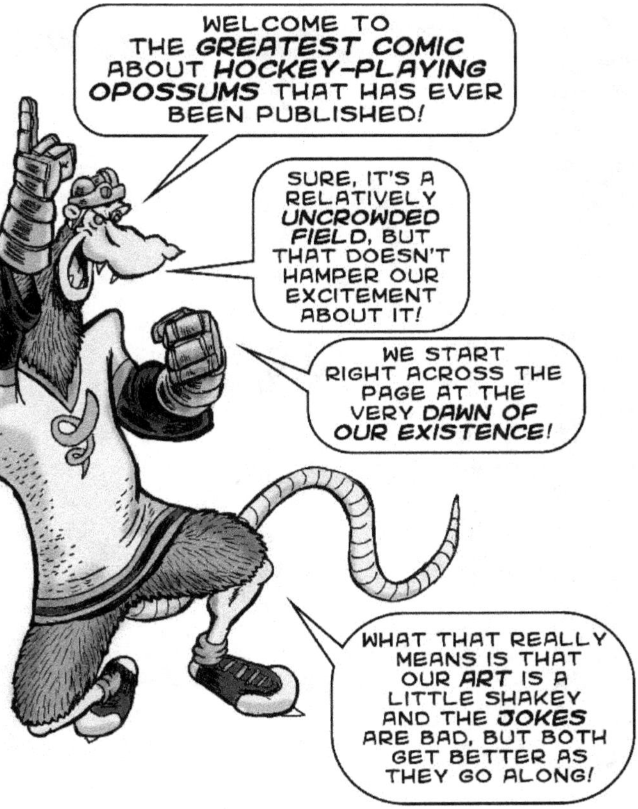

THE DOWNWARD SPIRALS BY JOHN SIMCOE

FINAL SCORE: DOWNWARD SPIRALS 2, DAM QUIXOTES 4

THE DOWNWARD SPIRALS

BY JOHN SIMCOE

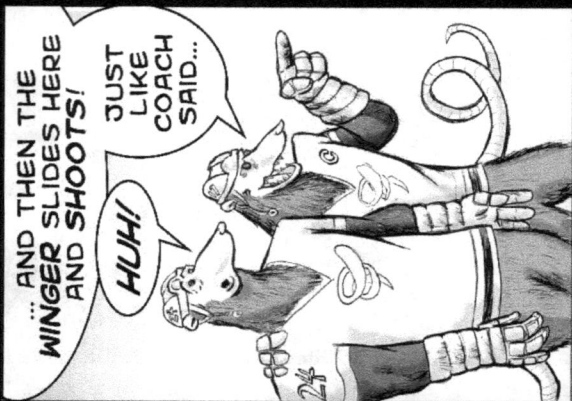

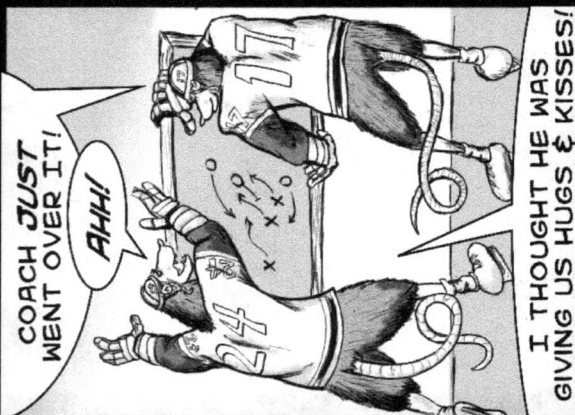

...AND THEN THE *WINGER* SLIDES HERE AND *SHOOTS!*

JUST LIKE COACH SAID...

HUH!

YEAH, BUT WHAT'S ALL THIS?

GRRR...

IT'S THE GAME PLAN!

COACH *JUST* WENT OVER IT!

AHH!

I THOUGHT HE WAS GIVING US HUGS & KISSES!

FINAL SCORE: DOWNWARD SPIRALS 2, MARSH INVADERS 3

THE DOWNWARD SPIRALS
BY JOHN SIMCOE

FINAL SCORE: DOWNWARD SPIRALS 2, APPLE CORPS 7

THE DOWNWARD SPIRALS BY JOHN SIMCOE

FINAL SCORE: DOWNWARD SPIRALS 2, BONE YARDS 3

THE DOWNNWARD SPIRALS BY JOHN SIMCOE

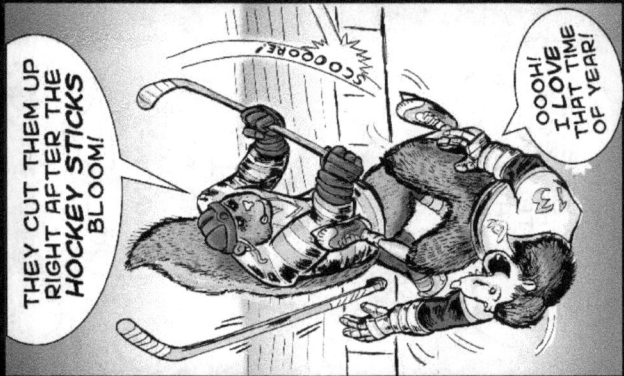

FINAL SCORE: DOWNWARD SPIRALS 1, BLUFF NUTS 6

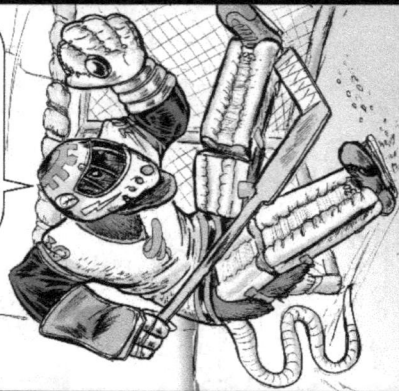

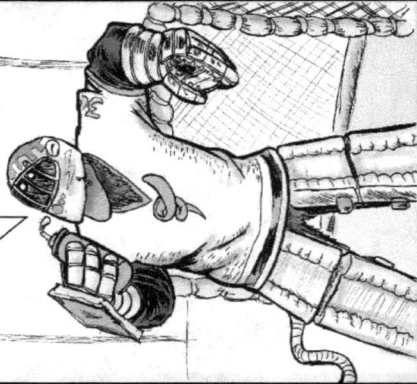

THE DOWNWARD SPIRALS BY JOHN SIMCOE

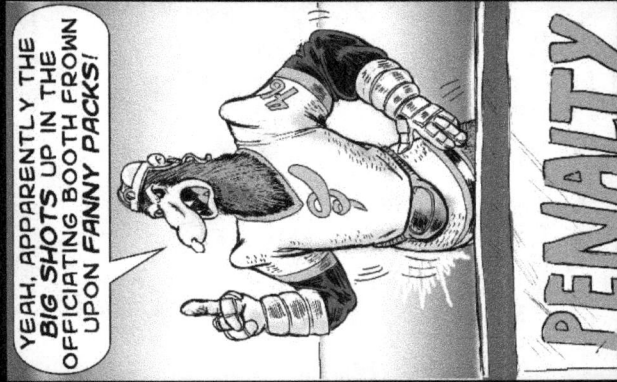

FINAL SCORE: DOWNWARD SPIRALS O, BRIDGE BILLIES 3

THE DOWNWARD SPIRALS BY JOHN SIMCOE

MAN, I *HATE* PLAYING ON A HOLIDAY!

WHO CARES, WE STILL GET PAID!

IT'S JUST THAT I GET FEELING ALL 'GUSHY' INSIDE.

I FEEL LIKE I GOTTA BE ALL *NICE* TO PEOPLE DURING THE HOLIDAYS.

SO JUST IMAGINE MY *OVERWHELMING* GUILT WHEN I GOTTA ...

... *KNOCK YOU OUT!*

UUGH!

FINAL SCORE: DOWNWARD SPIRALS 2, DAM QUIXOTES 4

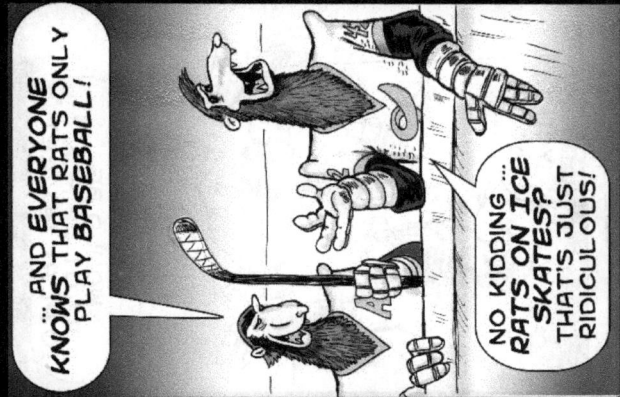

THE DOWNWARD SPIRALS BY JOHN SIMCOE

FINAL SCORE: DOWNWARD SPIRALS 2, APPLE CORPS 4

THE DOWNWARD SPIRALS BY JOHN SIMCOE

THE DOWNWARD SPIRALS BY JOHN SIMCOE

FINAL SCORE: DOWNWARD SPIRALS 0, BONE YARDS 3

THE DOWNWARD SPIRALS BY JOHN SIMCOE

FIGHTING WITH THE *GIRLFRIEND* ON LIVE TV?

NAW ... THAT'S "FINDING OUT YOU DIDN'T MAKE THE *THE ALL-STAR TEAM* ON LIVE TV!"

I DID *EVERYTHING* I COULD TO IMPRESS YOU!!

BUT IT WAS *NEVER* ENOUGH!

WAS I NOT GOOD ENOUGH?!?

AM I THAT TERRIBLE OF A OPOSSUM?

FINAL SCORE: DOWNWARD SPIRALS 2, BLUFF NUTS 4

THE DOWNWARD SPIRALS BY JOHN SIMCOE

AT THE BEGINNING OF A HOCKEY GAME, I LIKE TO BE THE ONE TO *SET THE TONE!*

JUST WATCH THIS ...

IF SOMETHING GOES WRONG TODAY, *YOU'RE THE ONE* WHO'S GONNA PAY FOR IT!

ME?!

AND WHAT IS THE *TONE* OF TODAY'S GAME?

I'M GONNA SAY *"BLACK AND BLUE."*

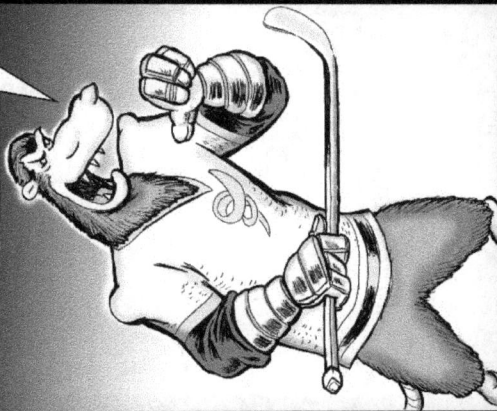

THE DOWNWARD SPIRALS   BY JOHN SIMCOE

UGH ... ANOTHER LOSS!

WE GOTTA DO SOMETHING TO GET BETTER!

LIKE WHAT?!

HOW ABOUT ...

WE GET ME TURNED INTO A *CYBORG!*

THE BIONIC OPOSSUM!!

"WE CAN REBUILD HIM!"

STRONGER! FASTER!

OF COURSE, THAT WOULD REQUIRE SOMETHING *AWFUL* TO HAPPEN TO ME.

WHAT'S THE BEST WAY TO GET IN A *PARACHUTING ACCIDENT?*

GO *PARA-CHUTING,* I'D BET.

FINAL SCORE: DOWNWARD SPIRALS 1, GARDEN JESTS 3

THE DOWNWARD SPIRALS   BY JOHN SIMCOE

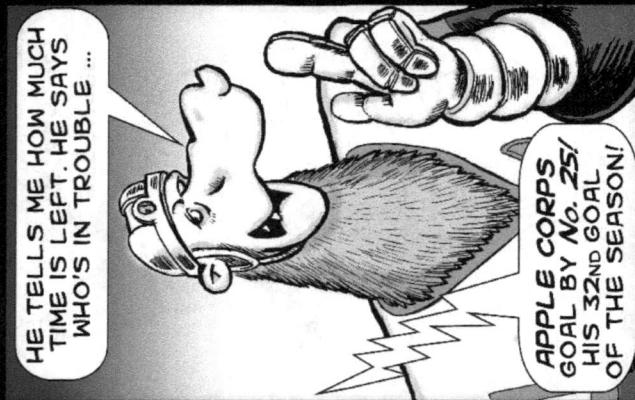

... AND WHO NEEDS TO BE *PUNISHED!!*

HE TELLS ME HOW MUCH TIME IS LEFT. HE SAYS WHO'S IN TROUBLE ...

APPLE CORPS GOAL BY *No. 25!* HIS 32ND GOAL OF THE SEASON!

TWO MINUTES LEFT IN THE PERIOD!

I FIND THE *VOICE FROM ABOVE* REASSURING.

HE'S *ALWAYS THERE* FOR ME.

FINAL SCORE: DOWNWARD SPIRALS O, APPLE CORPS 2

THE DOWNWARD SPIRALS BY JOHN SIMCOE

FINAL SCORE: DOWNWARD SPIRALS 0, LOCH FOXES 3

THE DOWNWARD SPIRALS BY JOHN SIMCOE

FINAL SCORE: DOWNWARD SPIRALS 2, BONE YARDS 4

THE DOWNWARD SPIRALS BY JOHN SIMCOE

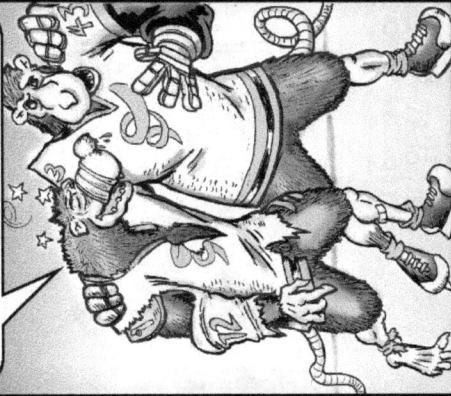

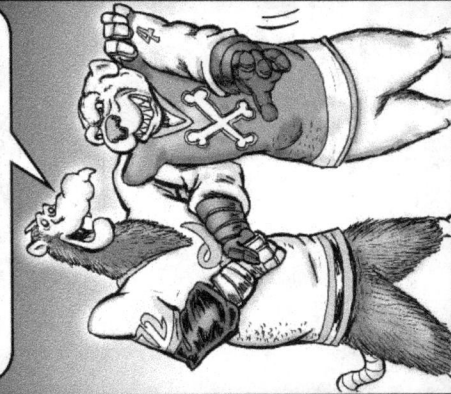

FINAL SCORE: DOWNWARD SPIRALS 1, BONE YARDS 4

THE DOWNWARD SPIRALS BY JOHN SIMCOE

FINAL SCORE: DOWNWARD SPIRALS 1, DAM QUIXOTES 3

THE DOWNWARD SPIRALS BY JOHN SIMCOE

FINAL SCORE: DOWNWARD SPIRALS 1, CONIFEROUS COLDBLOODS 0

THE DOWNWARD SPIRALS BY JOHN SIMCOE

FINAL SCORE: DOWNWARD SPIRALS 2, FINNISH LEMMINGS 7

THE DOWNWARD SPIRALS BY JOHN SIMCOE

FINAL SCORE: DOWNWARD SPIRALS 3, NORWAY RATS 5

Poodles vs Penguins
NATURAL ENEMIES AT WAR!
BY JOHN SIMCOE

Welcome to **Poodles vs. Penguins,** where natural enemies do battle to the bitter end!

What? Are we saying that **"Poodles hate Penguins"** and **"Penguins hate Poodles?"** Yes we are!

Just consider:

- Have you ever seen a poodle hanging out with a penguin?
- Poodles are from France (or some country like that) and Penguins are from Antarctica (or pretty darn close), why is it that they have to live so far apart?
- Poodles are dogs. Penguins are birds.
- Poodles need human help to look all fancy. Penguins look that way naturally. Jealous much?
- Penguins stink like dirty fish guts. Poodles smell like an alpine breeze wrapped in a roses. Now who's jealous?
- The first battle took place in Luxembourg. Why? Cuz nothing ever seems to happen in Luxembourg, so they figured that it would be a good place to start an international avian-canine conflict.
- Poodles were originally bred to kill rats. The penguins think that's pretty darn funny.
- Prehistoric penguins were six-feet tall. What happened between then and now?
- The second battle of the Poodle-Penguin War took place in Delaware. Why? Cuz nothing ever seems to happen in Delaware either.

GO TO THE NEXT PAGE FOR THIS TERRIBLE CONFLICT!

Poodles vs. Penguins No. 2
WAR CRIMES

Poodles vs. Penguins No. 3
SNEAK ATTACK

ABOUT THE AUTHOR!

JOHN SIMCOE has been cartooning, writing and drawing for fun most of his life. In fact, he has oodles of old sketchbooks that go back to his grade school years to prove it!

He came up with the concept for the **DOWNWARD SPIRALS** while visiting a local toy shop where he found an incredibly ugly puppet of an opossum. Somehow he started drawing them and then he started drawing them in hockey uniforms – the rest is history!

POODLES VS. PENGUINS came about after drawing a rather disturbing looking knife-wielding penguin on a piece of scrap paper. He has a lot more of that particular conflict to explore!

Simcoe lives in Pennsylvania with his wife, two kids, two cats, two hermit crabs and **absolutely no opossums, poodles or penguins.**

You can learn more about John and his thoughts on the world by visiting his website or linking up to him on social media!

ComicsontheBrain.com
Twitter: @johnsimcoe
Facebook: /TheJohnSimcoe
Email: John@johnsimcoe.com

www.ingramcontent.com/pod-product-compliance
Lightning Source LLC
Chambersburg PA
CBHW060631030426

42337CB00018B/3308